Charles Coombs

Hot-Air Balloning

illustrated with photographs

William Morrow and Company
New York 1981

Library of Congress Cataloging in Publication Data

Coombs, Charles Ira, 1914-
  Hot-air ballooning.

  Includes index.
  Summary: Traces the history of hot-air ballooning and describes the equipment, training and techniques of the successful aeronaut.
  1. Balloon ascensions—Juvenile literature. 2. Hot air balloons—Juvenile literature. [1. Balloon ascensions. 2. Hot air balloons] I. Title.
GV762.C66   797.5   80-26704
ISBN 0-688-00364-8
ISBN 0-688-00365-6 (lib. bdg.)

Photo credits

All photographs are by the author with the exception of the following: *Ballooning Magazine*, pp. 6, 18, 33, 37, 42, 43, 88, 112, 114, 115, 117, 118, 121; Rob Burbach, p. 109; Goodyear Aerospace Corp., pp. 28, 29, 30, 32, 113; Will Hayes, p. 40; Dick Kent, pp. 35, 36; Don Piccard, pp. 12, 20, 99; Raven Industries Inc., pp. 44, 54. Permission is gratefully acknowledged.

Contents

Foreword

Upnzway. When I saw those letters on the license plate of the chase vehicle, I had a hunch that exploring the world of ballooning was going to be fun as well as exciting. And from the moment I sat down with Richard Swercewski ("Just call me Ski") and Rob Burbach, it was both.

Ski and Rob are coowners of the *Caliente*, a towering, rainbow-hued Raven AX-7 hot-air balloon. The first day we were together they invited me aloft, and from there on the adventure soared. One day we skimmed across a small lake without getting our feet wet, and then we lifted and drifted quietly over the awakening desert. Another time we joined the ground crew chasing desperately after the balloon, which was being carried seaward by an unexpected wind. The pilot did manage finally to put down before reaching the water. We shared coffee and doughnuts while waiting for sunrise when the balloon could take to the air.

The spirit of fun and excitement prevailed wherever I went in pursuit of ballooning knowledge. Don Piccard, famous son of a famous ballooning family, showed me how hot-air balloon systems are made, and he patiently explained the way that they function.

A surprise call from Brian Lawler, editor of *Ballooning*, a bimonthly journal, set up a meeting that was enormously rewarding in both data and pictures.

Everyone I met was most willing to help me gather information and provide pictures that escaped my own camera. If hot air makes a balloon rise, the enthusiasm of those I came in contact with—pilot, crew, passengers, or manufacturers of balloons—helps keep it aloft.

To all those people who made my research such a pleasure, many thanks, and up-up-and-away!

Charles "Chick" Coombs
Westlake Village, California, 1981

1
The First Flights

As long as men and women have walked the earth they have envied the birds and tried to emulate their flying. Sometimes the results were comic, sometimes tragic. Eventually manned flight was accomplished, however, and it began with balloons. People found they could ride aloft attached to bubbles filled with hot air or lightweight gases.

In the third century B.C., a Greek mathematician named Archimedes summed up the principle of ballooning: When a gas that is less dense than air is enclosed in a container, the difference between the density of the gas and that of the air it displaces causes the container to rise.

A balloon flies because the widely separated molecules of a thin gas such as hydrogen or helium, or of the heated air that expands inside the bag, are less dense

9

and thus lighter than those of the air outside the bag. In attempting to rise or escape from its confinement, the buoyant lightweight gas or heated air lifts the balloon along with it.

How Archimedes was able to arrive at this principle is open to speculation. After all, there are no examples of lighter-than-air vehicles in nature. Normally, whatever soars skyward does so by virtue of its aerodynamic design. Like an airplane, it is lifted by the effect of outside forces, usually wind, upon its surface. It does not soar because it is ·lighter than the surrounding atmosphere. Even a feather in the breeze is an aerodynamic form. It flies solely by the force of air currents playing upon it. If the breeze stops, the feather slowly floats to earth.

On the other hand, a balloon's buoyancy is static, not dependent on a dynamic force such as wind or motor. A balloon rises because it is filled with gas or heated air that is thinner in density and thus lighter in weight than the surrounding atmosphere. A bubble rises in water for the same reasons.

Because of this static, or self-sustaining, lift, a balloon is sometimes called an "aerostat," and the science

For centuries ballooning has inspired fantastical ideas.

10

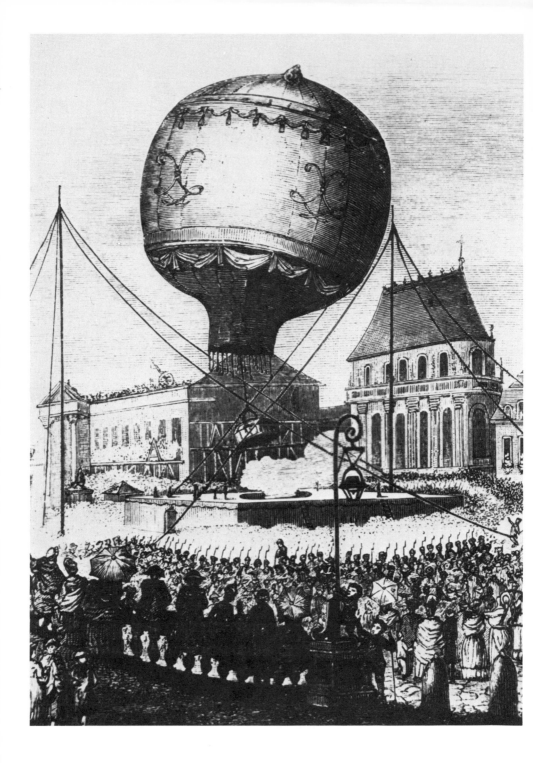

of ballooning "aerostation." Balloonists also may be called "aeronauts," from the Greek words *aéro* (of the air) and *nautēs* (sailor). Usually, however, the vehicles are referred to as balloons or lighter-than-air (LTA) craft, and their operation is simply known as ballooning. Whether the pilot is referred to as an aeronaut or a balloonist is a matter of preference. Any of the terms are acceptable.

Ancient Peruvian artifacts, old Chinese tales, and other historic evidence give hints that balloons, or at least small, man-made objects resembling balloons, probably existed thousands of years ago. But there is no concrete proof as the written history of ballooning dates back a scant two centuries to the experiments of two French brothers named Joseph and Étienne Montgolfier. The Montgolfiers were intrigued by the bits of scrap paper that soared up their chimney along with the smoke from their fireplace. Assuming that the smoke was doing the lifting, they began making lightweight paper spheres, open at the mouth. They held the small aerostats over a smoking fire until the spheres were filled with enough smoke to rise toward the ceiling.

Aviation began with the successful lift-off
of the first Montgolfier balloon over Paris in 1783.

Delighted with their discovery, the brothers secretly made and flew an assortment of small, smoke-filled paper balloons. They became enthralled with the possibilities of aerostation and visualized many ways that balloons might be put to use.

Finally they decided to bring aerostation to public attention. The Montgolfiers then sewed together a large sphere of linen cloth, lining it with paper to keep the smoke from escaping through the porous material. The final sphere was 33 feet in diameter and had a 22,000 cubic foot smoke capacity.

On June 4, 1783, on a public square at Annonay, France, the Montgolfiers piled damp straw beneath the open throat of the cloth-and-paper bag. They added rags, leather scraps, anything that would produce lots of smoke when burned. (Only later did the Montgolfiers realize that the heated air, not the smoke, was what caused their balloons to rise.) When they lit the pile of fuel and heat surged up into the balloon, it swayed and started to rise. At that point, Étienne called for volunteers from the crowd to help hold it down. Seeing that the flames were getting dangerously close to the fabric, Joseph yelled, "Hands off!" The volunteers let go of the balloon, and amid gasps from the spectators the large, unmanned aerostat lifted ponderously. It climbed steadily to an astounding altitude of about six thousand feet. Then it drifted northward, pushed by a gentle breeze. Within ten minutes the balloon had cooled and started to descend. It landed about a mile and a half from where the flight began.

At the same time that the Montgolfiers were experimenting with hot-air balloons, a young Parisian scientist named Jacques Charles was testing balloons filled with a light gas. The gas had been discovered in 1766 by an English scientist named Henry Cavendish. Seven times lighter than air and quite explosive, the new gas was called "phlogiston" or "inflammable air." Years later it became known as hydrogen, the lightest of the elements.

An early problem for Charles was that the thin hydrogen gas quickly escaped through the flimsy silk fabric of his balloon. He recruited the help of brothers Jean and Noël Robert, who developed a method of varnishing the silk to make it gas-tight while retaining the needed lightness and flexibility.

On August 27, 1783, after having laboriously generated sufficient hydrogen by trickling sulfuric acid over a bed of iron filings, Charles released his balloon from the outskirts of Paris. There were loud cheers from the crowd, most of whom had been charged admission to help defray expenses.

The aerostat had a twelve-foot diameter—much smaller than that of the Montgolfiers' hot-air balloon. Nevertheless, it climbed steadily to an altitude of three thousand feet, got caught in a rainstorm, and floated sixteen miles into the country before it fell back to earth. Thinking it was some evil object from outer space, the frightened and hostile peasants attacked the flimsy envelope with clubs and pitchforks.

Despite such uncertain beginnings, ballooning captivated the imagination and enthusiasm of people all over the civilized world. Many scientists turned their thoughts toward manned flight and other serious applications of ballooning. But because they did not understand the mysteries of the upper atmosphere, they did not know whether human beings could survive high up in the sky.

As a preliminary test, the Montgolfiers released a hot-air balloon carrying a crew composed of a duck, a rooster, and a sheep. After an eight-minute flight, the balloon cooled and descended, returning the first live aeronauts back to earth. The only casualty was a broken wing on the rooster, which had been stepped on by the sheep in her excitement.

Greatly encouraged, the Montgolfiers requested

permission from Louis XVI of France to send a man aloft. The request was denied. Then François Pilâtre de Rozier, a young scientist of the court, convinced the king that he was not afraid and wished to have the great honor of being the first person to fly. Hesitantly the king consented, but he ordered that the balloon be tethered with a rope so it would not drift away and could be pulled back if anything went amiss.

In mid-October, 1783, Pilâtre de Rozier climbed onto the platform that had been built around the open throat of the balloon. Although formerly the hot air had been generated in a ground-based fire pit set up under the balloon, this time the Montgolfiers attached a basketlike metal firepan to the balloon itself, centering it beneath the open mouth of the sphere. The grate was designed to carry a straw-fed fire and provide steady heat during the flight.

On their first tethered flight, the balloon ascended to only about eighty feet due to a rather short rope. Yet the young scientist was having his problems. Standing alone on one side of the ring-shaped platform, he saw that the aerostat was tipping dangerously off-balance. After being up for about five minutes with flames licking toward the fabric of the tilting aerostat, Pilâtre de Rozier signaled to be pulled down.

The Montgolfier brothers also had noted the prob-

lem. For the next flight, they gathered up enough rocks in a sack to match Pilâtre de Rozier's weight and put the ballast on the opposite side of the platform from Pilâtre de Rozier. The ascension was then an unqualified success.

On following days they made more captive flights at ever-increasing altitudes. Most were without incident. Accordingly, the Montgolfiers figured the time had come to take off the tethers and try free flight.

On November 20, 1783, Pilâtre de Rozier and a courtier named the Marquis d'Arlandes attempted the first truly free manned flight in a balloon. Under cloudy skies they climbed onto the ringlike platform of a brand-new, gaily decorated Montgolfier, which had become the name for all hot-air balloons. (Similarly the name of Charlier, derived from Jacques Charles, came to be used for a gas-filled aerostat. These terms are still common in some of today's ballooning circles.)

Before a crowd estimated to be over 400,000, which included the king and queen of France, the two men soared aloft from the crown prince's spacious chateau gardens outside of Paris. They kept feeding straw to the fire as they climbed. The balloon ascended to a height

Eighteenth century aerostation was used
to decorate artifacts of the age.

of some five hundred feet, floated over Paris, and landed safely a half hour later on the far outskirts of town.

Within two weeks a Charlier lifted off from Paris, carrying Charles and Noël Robert on a two-hour, twenty-five-mile flight that ended in a pasture outside the city.

A few months later, a cheerful young lady named Madame Thible ascended in a Montgolfier from Lyons, France, singing merrily all the way, and became the first free-ballooning woman aeronaut. Soaring balloons, both gas-filled and hot-air-filled, were soon the rage of Europe.

The age of manned flight had arrived.

The teardrop shape of hot-air balloons
has changed little over the centuries.

2
Gas Versus
Hot Air

Less expensive and simpler in concept than gas-filled aerostats, hot-air balloons nevertheless require a steady source of heat to stay aloft. During the late 1700's, the needed heat usually was provided by burning straw or other material. This process was cumbersome, unreliable, and dangerous at best, and hot-air ballooning was soon restricted to entertainment. It had little practical worth in cross-country or high-altitude flights.

Clearly hydrogen-filled balloons were more reliable if not necessarily safer than the Montgolfiers. A balloonist could control a Charlier's flight—as much as any balloon flight could be controlled—by dropping

A balloon moves with the wind,
despite efforts to control its direction.

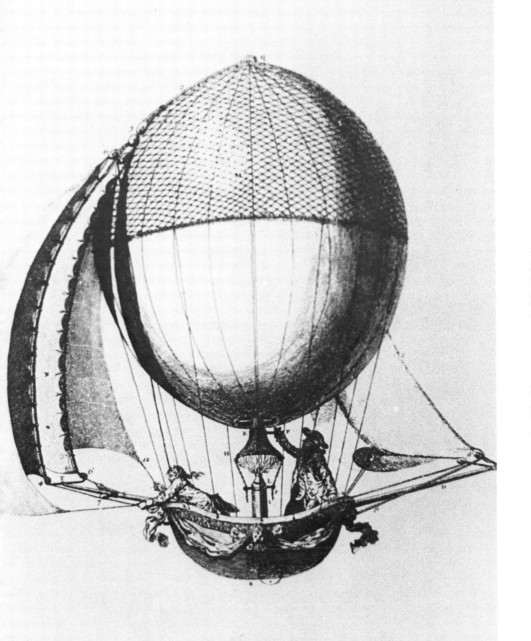

sand or water ballast in order to rise and releasing hydrogen gas in order to descend. A flight could continue until the ballast was gone or until there was not enough hydrogen left in the bag to keep it buoyant. Then the flight quickly came to an end.

As balloon manufacturing flourished, an interest in ballooning spread to many parts of the world. A noted French aeronaut named Jean Pierre Blanchard took his gas bag to England, where he met a wealthy American doctor named John Jeffries. Dr. Jeffries agreed to finance Blanchard's dream of ballooning across the English Channel to France provided he could go along. Since Blanchard couldn't make the try without money, he consented.

On January 7, 1785, the two men took off from the British shore with favorable westerly winds and headed in the general direction of France. Halfway across the Channel, the balloon began to lose its lift and dropped toward the sea. Blanchard and Jeffries frantically released all the ballast. Finally, as the basket dipped into the water, they threw out everything else that was loose, including part of their clothing. Happily, the aerostat rose once again, drifted serenely on over the French coastline, and came down a dozen miles inland.

Blanchard made many other flights around Europe,

introducing ballooning to Germany, Holland, Belgium, and Poland. Then, in late 1792, he packed up his balloon and sailed for the United States.

Soon after his arrival, January 9, 1793, Blanchard made an ascension with a hydrogen-filled balloon from a prison yard in Philadelphia, then the nation's capital. In his pocket Blanchard carried a letter of introduction from President George Washington in case he got lost or landed among unfriendly people.

As the balloon climbed, Blanchard looked down at the sea of upturned faces and relished the cheers floating up to him in the still morning air. Drifting on a southerly breeze, he crossed the broad Delaware River and was soon over New Jersey. Within less than an hour, he decided to descend, released some of the hydrogen, and landed near the town of Woodbury, fifteen miles from the capital.

Americans quickly took to ballooning, though in most instances it remained an amusing novelty. There were those, however, who began seeking more serious applications of aerostation. In 1794, France organized the world's first balloon corps for duty in fighting against Germany, Holland, and Austria. Its members were known as Aerostiers. At the battle of Fleurus, the corpsmen went aloft in tethered observation balloons to look across enemy lines. They took notes and then used elaborate semaphore signals to direct firepower against their opponents. Fleurus fell, and the French soon surged on towards Brussels.

Flushed with victory, the Aerostiers persuaded Napoleon to allow them to go against the English during the Egyptian campaign in 1798. But the British were well prepared, and they quickly destroyed most of the balloons and support equipment. Distraught and suddenly quite distrustful of the worth of balloons, Napoleon sent the Aerostiers home.

No further effort was made to use balloons in wartime until the American Civil War in 1861. With the approval of President Abraham Lincoln, a young inventor named Thaddeus Lowe fabricated an assortment of gas-filled balloons. Like the French in Fleurus, he controlled them with long rope tethers. When corpsmen were posted high aloft in the balloon baskets, they could scan distances up to fifty miles. Professor Lowe also rigged up a telegraph line leading from the balloon directly to the president's office, and he developed a signal system to direct ground-based artillery fire at unseen enemies.

Hearing of Professor Lowe's work, a German count named Ferdinand von Zeppelin came to visit him.

Von Zeppelin had long been interested in developing a balloon that could be propelled and guided, not just flown according to the will of the winds.

Various attempts had already been made. In Europe, a few elongated balloons with simple rudders had been built. Some aeronauts had attempted to row their balloons through the air with feathered oars. Steam engines were tried too. But all these methods were unsuccessful. The steam engines, for example, were much too heavy for the amount of propeller power they produced.

At the end of the nineteenth century, however, light-weight gasoline-fueled internal-combustion engines were developed. Their availability gave new impetus to power ballooning. In Germany, Count von Zeppelin launched his first true airship in 1900. It was a 420-foot-long, cigar-shaped, rigid aluminum structure that housed seventeen individual hydrogen-filled bags. Slung beneath the metal-braced envelope were an open gondola and two sixteen-horsepower marine engines. Called the Luftschiff Zeppelin No. 1 (LZ-1), the giant airship made one short flight and crashed.

Not long thereafter, on December 17, 1903, the Wright brothers flew the first heavier-than-air machine off the sand dunes of Kitty Hawk, North Carolina.

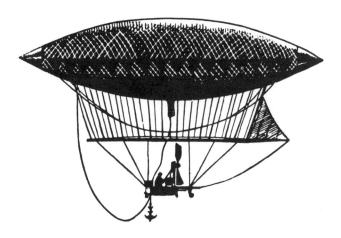

By the mid-1800s a crude power-driven balloon
had been built and flown.

The age of full-powered, high-speed aviation was under
way, and almost overnight the more erratic free-flying
balloons were all but forgotten.

But not entirely. Count von Zeppelin hadn't given
up with the crash of the LZ-1. He continued building
the rigid airships, which the French had started calling
"dirigibles," meaning "capable of being directed."

With the advent of World War I, a number of German zeppelins were sent across the Channel to drop
bombs upon England. When the British airplane pilots
adapted and began shooting down the hydrogen-filled
craft with flaming incendiary bullets, however, the balloon attacks ceased.

Following the war, Dr. Hugo Eckener, who had taken control of the zeppelin works, flew a newly built airship to Lakehurst, New Jersey, and presented it to the United States Navy as a part of German reparations. Renamed the *Los Angeles*, the giant craft flew hundreds of trips over a period of eight years, until she was decommissioned in 1932.

Not so happy, however, was the fate of most other dirigibles. Both in the United States and in Europe, they were beset by bad weather or structural failure and crashed or broke up one after another. In April, 1933, the large American-built U.S.S. *Akron* ran into a violent squall off the coast of New Jersey and was lost at

One of the largest American airships, the ill-fated *Akron* was 785 feet long and filled with 6,500,000 cubic feet of helium.

A nonrigid airship, the familiar Goodyear blimp is
a modern remnant of the age of dirigibles.

sea with seventy-four of its crew of seventy-eight. Other
zeppelin disasters were all too frequent.

Of the large dirigibles that were used to carry passengers and cargo, only the *Graf Zeppelin* emerged un-
scathed. From the end of World War I until her retire-
ment in 1937, the *Graf* made 590 commercial flights
totaling some 17,000 hours of flying time and covering
over a million miles. She carried some 40,000 passengers plus many tons of freight, and she crossed the
Atlantic Ocean 144 times without serious accident.

The *Graf* was quickly followed by a bigger and more modern airship, the *Hindenburg*. A magnificent dirigible, the *Hindenburg* was more than 800 feet long, almost three times the length of a standard football field. She had an airspeed of nearly eighty miles per hour, a range of 8000 miles, and luxurious accommodations for seventy-two passengers. The *Hindenburg's* main route was between Germany and the United States. With favorable weather, and pushed along by four 1100-horsepower Mercedes-Benz diesel engines, she could make the crossing in two days.

But the *Hindenburg*, like most other foreign-made dirigibles of the time, relied on inflammable hydrogen for her buoyancy. Helium, an inert, safer, nonexplosive gas, was not available to the Germans in the quantities needed.

On May 6, 1937, while nudging toward the docking tower at Lakehurst, New Jersey, the *Hindenburg* mysteriously burst into flame. Consumed in a ball of fire, the airship crashed to the ground. Passengers and crew members jumped from the blazing inferno as best they could. Within less than a minute, the stately dirigible was a heap of twisted metal and charred ruins. Thirteen passengers and twenty crewmen died. The era of the giant rigid airships had come to an end.

Most ballooning that took place during the next several decades was exploratory in nature. Lightweight plastic films were used to make enormous gas bags. These bags carried scientific instruments aloft or lifted pressurized gondolas, which enabled men and women to ascend safely to heights of well beyond 100,000 feet.

But now gas ballooning had become increasingly expensive. The big bags and gondolas were costly, and a balloon full of helium, which had largely supplanted

Free-flying gas balloons have probed
the mysteries of the outer atmosphere.

Though an expensive operation,
gas ballooning still has its devotees.

the far more dangerous hydrogen, could run into thousands of dollars. With orbiting satellites and high-flying fixed-wing aircraft available, the Government had little use for exploratory gas balloons. The few that remained were used primarily for sport.

A landmark achievement of gas ballooning was still to come, however. In August, 1978, three prosperous and courageous New Mexico businessmen lifted off from Presque Isle, Maine, in an open boat-shaped gondola hanging beneath an eleven-story-high, neoprene-coated nylon, helium-filled balloon envelope. Traveling on wind power alone, they started across the Atlantic Ocean. They dodged storms and sought favorable westerly winds at altitudes varying from 4000 to nearly 25,000 feet. During the entire flight they controlled their altitude by delicately balancing the release of ballast with the release of helium. When both ballast and helium were running low, the three adventurers brought the aerostat down in a barley field near Miserey, France, on the evening of August 17. The distance covered was an estimated 3120 miles, and they had been in the air for almost six days and nights (137 hours, 3 minutes.)

The great challenge of crossing the Atlantic Ocean in a balloon had been met. This aerostat, called the *Double Eagle II*, now rests in the National Air and

Dangling a hang glider that had to be jettisoned
during a crucial stage of the flight, *Double Eagle II*
soars high over the Atlantic Ocean.

The *Double Eagle II* aeronauts, with their medals,
after their record-breaking balloon flight to France.

Space Museum in Washington, D.C. Its flight might
well mark the ultimate in gas-bag ballooning for years
to come, although there are people who dream of non-
stop around-the-world flights.

During these years, advances were also taking place
in hot-air ballooning, and as far back as the early 1960s
it had begun to regain its popularity. The major factor
in its revival was the introduction of inexpensive propane fuel and efficient, lightweight, portable burners.
With this equipment, the heat needed to keep a hot-air
balloon aloft could be produced more easily.

36

Soon growing numbers of Americans were taking to the skies in wicker baskets or aluminum gondolas hung beneath bulbous, open-throated, nylon envelopes. In a very short time the United States became the leader in both the manufacture and the use of these rainbow-hued aerostats.

A new age of hot-air ballooning had arrived.

Modern-day ballooning is mostly of the hot-air variety.

3

Construction

There are fewer than a dozen commercial hot-air-balloon manufacturers in the world. These companies produce a vast majority of the flamboyantly colored spheres seen drifting through the skies on calm, clear days. Only a few balloons are made by individuals, families, or ballooning clubs.

Whatever their source, balloons are legally classified as aircraft, along with Piper Cubs and Boeing 747s. Like these larger machines, they come under the jurisdiction of the Federal Aviation Administration (FAA). Each balloon must undergo a thorough inspection and earn an FAA Airworthiness Certificate before it is allowed to fly. It must be registered and licensed like any other aircraft. An aerostat that is improperly made or poorly maintained will not be allowed off the ground.

Aloft or on the ground, a balloon is sure to draw attention.

Among the more familiar brands of hot-air balloons are Raven, Piccard, Barnes, Adams, Eagle, and Cameron. Although each manufacturer follows a basic plan, there are many variations in design and manufacturing techniques.

A hot-air balloon is far more complex than the multicolored envelope suggests. It is a complete system, and its major components are the envelope, fuel tanks, burner, basket, and instruments. How well these parts

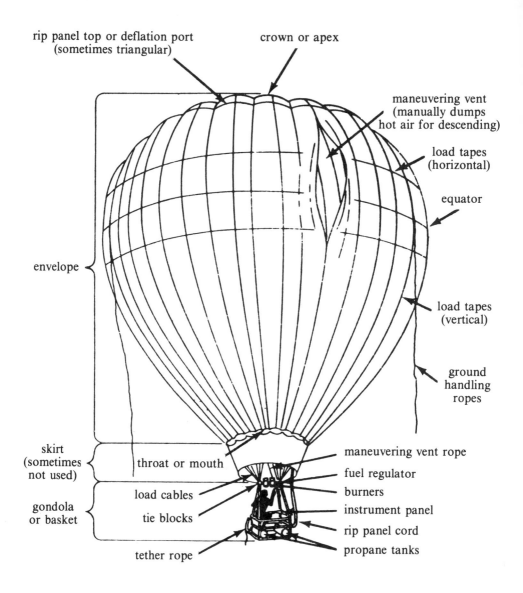

The basic makeup of a hot-air balloon.

40

are designed, engineered, and assembled determines how effective, durable, and safe the balloon will be.

The construction of a balloon begins with careful planning. The first decision to be made is about size. What size will best suit the aeronaut's needs?

All free-flying aerostats carry a basic identifying letter *A*. Those that have only the single letter are gas-filled balloons while those marked *AX* are hot-air balloons. The hot-air balloons are further graded from one through ten according to cubic-foot capacity. A small AX-1 aerostat, of around 25,000 cubic feet, is just large enough to carry a fairly light person dangling in a special harness or straddling the small propane tank needed to fuel the burner. A large, bulbous AX-10 may contain more than 200,000 cubic feet of hot air, and it is capable of lifting several thousand pounds of passengers and other payload.

The most popular sizes are AX-5 (40,000 cubic feet), AX-6 (58,000 cubic feet), AX-7 (77,000 cubic feet), and AX-8 (88,000 cubic feet). The larger balloons carry two to four passengers, plus tanks, equipment, and instruments. They are the favorites for sport ballooning, promotional work, and public rides.

The second step is to choose the colors and draw the design of the envelope. The more vivid the hues, the

An AX-1 compared to an AX-7.

better, and the range runs from vibrant orange to lush green, sunny yellow, and fiery red.

The colors are combined in a pattern such as climbing swirls, herringbone slashes, complicated checkerboards, or stripes. Indeed, a carefully designed Alpine landscape may completely encircle the envelope. A balloonist's self-created design is as individual as a jockey's silks or a cattleman's brand. It is respected by other aeronauts and seldom copied. The design is done on a simple chart that the manufacturer follows as he translates it into nylon or Dacron balloon fabric.

Envelope decorative schemes vary widely.

The next step is the actual fabrication of the envelope. Balloon shapes vary according to the manufacturer, but usually a balloon is made up of elongated panels, or gores, of thin, strong, heat-resistant nylon or Dacron stitched together into a pear-shaped sphere. Each gore carefully follows the color chart. Often the gore is made up of many individual pieces that are sewn together to add strength and provide a pleasing roundness to the envelope when it is inflated.

Ample space and machinery are needed
for fabricating balloon envelopes.

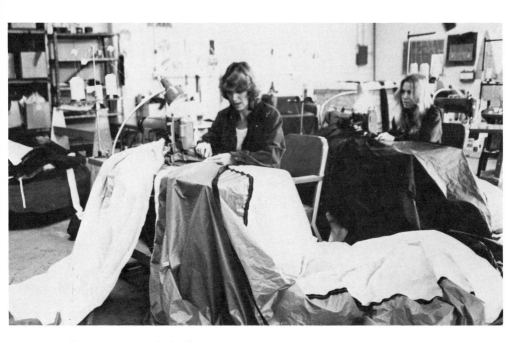

Seamstresses stitch the gores
that make up the bulb-shaped envelope.

The pieces of material that make up the gores are piled one atop the other in stacks on a long cutting table. They are then cut with an electric knife according to patterns. These sections are sorted and numbered on the corners to guide the sewing-machine operators.

The operator matches numbers and proceeds to stitch the individually designed pieces together on a heavy-duty sewing machine threaded with strong polyester thread. One completed gore is then added to another until, like orange slices, the pieces fit together in a sphere.

During the sewing, however, other things take place. The nylon fabric and the stitched seams in themselves might not be strong enough to support the burner assembly, the gondola, and the eventual payload. So strong webbed nylon load tapes are added along each seam. Not only do the tapes support the weight of whatever will hang beneath the balloon, they take the strain off the fabric itself. A few additional horizontal load tapes may be sewed around the balloon's midsection, or equator, to help prevent the balloon from bursting under internal pressure. This strengthening also helps maintain the spherical shape of the bag.

A maneuvering vent is added during the sewing too. It is basically a self-sealing opening, or slot, positioned high up on the envelope and is operated by a pull rope that reaches down through the bag to the pilot's station in the basket. Its main purpose is to get rid of excessive hot air, giving the pilot more control of the descent. The cooler the air inside becomes, the faster the balloon descends. The maneuvering vent has little effect upon the lateral, or sideways, movement of the balloon, which is subject to the whims of the wind.

The all-important rip panel, or deflation port, also is sewn into the top of the balloon. Usually, it is the plug of fabric that makes up the crown itself. Or it

Looking through a partially inflated balloon
toward the open rip panel in the crown.

might be a triangular panel that starts at the top and stretches down toward the balloon's equator. Sometimes for added stability in case of high altitude deflation, parachuting features are built into the rip panel. Held in place by Velcro friction fasteners, the rip panel is activated by a red-coded strap hanging within reach of the pilot. The pilot yanks this tape during any landings when he or she wants to spill the air from the envelope quickly to prevent the balloon from being dragged by the wind.

Finally, strong steel cables or heavy ropes are fastened to the lower tips of the load tapes. These cables support the burner assembly and the gondola itself.

Meanwhile, in another part of the plant, the fuel system is assembled. This system is composed of tanks, valves, gauges, regulators, burners, and the assorted fuel lines that connect all the parts.

Both stainless-steel and aluminum propane tanks are commonly used in hot-air balloons. For ease in handling, tank capacity generally ranges from ten to twenty gallons. Two or more tanks are usually carried during a flight. The liquid propane is piped to the burners mounted on a frame just beneath the open mouth of the balloon.

Most balloons have one or two burners; a few use as

Hot-air ballooning depends upon
properly assembled burner systems.

many as four burner cans or pots in a cluster. The
number depends largely upon the size of the balloon
and on the amount of heat that can be generated by a
single burner.

Above or around the can is a coil in which the liquified petroleum gas (LPG), or propane, is converted to

vapor before being fed into the burner nozzles. As it spews from the nozzles, the propane mixes with oxygen in the air to become a flammable fuel. A built-in pilot light and a hand-operated throttle called a "blast valve" provide instant full-power heat when needed. In addition to the blast valve, there is an adjustable regulator valve, or cruise valve, that can be used when a lower even heat and less noise are desired.

The burners may be mounted on a free-floating rack that hangs from the load cables connecting the envelope and the basket. Or they may be gimbaled to rotate and mounted on a rigid frame attached to the gondola. In either case, the burners are centered beneath the open mouth of the balloon, where the blast of heat will shoot directly and forcibly up into the bag without searing the edges of the envelope.

The basket, or gondola, is the third major component of the hot-air balloon. From the very first manned flights, balloon baskets have been woven of wicker. This material remains traditional for good reason. It is both strong and flexible, which makes it able to absorb the shock of occasional rough landings.

One favored wicker comes from Borneo, where a particular species of ground ivy grows. When properly cured, it makes a very strong, nonsplintering rattan.

Customarily, balloon baskets are woven of rattan.

Skilled weavers carefully braid the soaked rattan around a hardwood frame built atop a solid wood platform that is supported on skids. Sometimes a lightweight metal frame is used.

The waist-high basket is perhaps three or four feet square, just big enough to carry three or four people, propane tanks, instruments, and other needed items.

The padded basket rim is edged with soft leather to make hanging on or climbing over easier. Often a thick leather scuff guard is placed around the bottom of the gondola to protect the wicker from damage when the basket tips or is dragged sideways during a windy landing.

Some modern-day balloonists reject the traditional wicker, and their baskets are constructed of aluminum tubing or molded fiber-glass panels.

An instrument package rounds out the basic balloon system. Like all equipment in hot-air ballooning, it is light and simple. Thus, only three instruments are considered essential, although some aeronauts add others. The main instrument package consists of an altimeter to measure the balloon's height above the ground, a variometer, or vertical-speed indicator, that measures the rate of climb or descent in feet-per-minute, and a temperature indicator, or pyrometer,

A sports balloonist's basic flight instrument
package contains a vertical speed indicator,
a heat-sensitive pyrometer, and an altimeter.

that reads the all-important air temperature in the
crown of the aerostat, the hottest and so most critical
area.

These three instruments usually are contained in a
small, portable package that can be hooked over the
rim of the basket or mounted elsewhere during flight.
When not in use, it can be stored in a protective box.

A compass comes in handy for seeking whatever
favorable breezes have been forecast. For instance,
when checking with a Flight Service Station (FSS) before takeoff, a pilot may be told that a moderate

A few hot-air balloons, like dirigibles,
are steerable and power-driven.

westerly wind probably will be encountered at an altitude of about twenty-five hundred feet. By checking his compass and noting that open fields for a safe landing lie to the east, he may add burner heat and climb to take advantage of the westerly.

A compass along with a map may also be useful after a forced landing in some remote area.

Many aeronauts carry some sort of communication equipment as well. They may have a simple short-range walkie-talkie, a citizen's band (CB) radio, or the more sophisticated and expensive FM frequency communications package. Each enables the aeronaut to stay in contact with the chase vehicle that follows somewhere below, trying to keep the balloon in sight.

Actually, the chase vehicle must be considered a basic part of any balloon system too. Operated by ground-crew members, the chase vehicle may be a station wagon, a pickup truck, or a camper towing a small trailer. It can be any wheeled vehicle with the capacity to haul the folded-up nylon envelope, basket, extra fuel tanks, passengers, and the other necessities of ballooning.

The size and variety of the bags and the components that make up a hot-air balloon are endless. There are even thermal dirigibles, which resemble blimps, but use hot air instead of helium for lift. Equipped with a small propeller-turning combustion engine and a rudder, they can cruise the sky at a speed of about ten miles per hour.

Regardless of size, design, or cost, all aerostats share a common purpose—to provide the balloonist with the pleasantest experience possible.

4
Training and Safety

The pilot is master over all operations that take place during a balloon flight, but success depends upon the combined efforts of several people working closely together. Most ballooning, in fact, is a group activity, and many balloons are owned by clubs.

A hot-air balloon may cost anywhere between four and forty thousand dollars. Most in the mid-AX range commonly seen drifting through the weekend skies cost from about six to twelve thousand dollars complete, too expensive for most individuals. Property liability, personal injury insurance, plus coverage on the balloon itself adds to the overall price. A club, therefore, is a practical way to share the cost.

Although most club members aspire to become pilots in time, they must first serve an apprenticeship in the ground crew in order to learn the fundamentals

An aspiring balloonist may tote tanks
as part of his apprenticeship.

of hot-air ballooning. Of course, each such group is formed around the nucleus of at least one certified, experienced pilot.

Since a balloon is an aircraft in the eyes of the Federal Aviation Administration, a balloonist must earn his or her license in much the same manner as the pilot of a fixed-wing airplane or helicopter. In general, that is, the applicant must know and abide by the rules detailed in Part 61 of the Federal Aviation Regulations, known as FAR-61. Due to the less complicated and demanding nature of free ballooning, however, the requirements have been considerably modified. So it is much easier to become a licensed balloonist than a licensed airplane pilot.

There are three classes of balloon pilots in the United States: student, private, and commercial. One usually leads to the other. A student pilot must be at least fourteen years old. The applicant need not undergo a physical examination, but he or she must certify to not having any medical defect that might interfere with piloting a free balloon. Although not required, many wisely take a basic examination and obtain a Third Class Medical clearance.

Since communication is such an important part of aerostation, the student must be able to read, speak, and understand English. The student also should be familiar with Part 91 of the Federal Aviation Regulations. This code contains the general operating and flight rules to which all airborne vehicles in the United States are subject.

An aeronaut must be able to control the crowd
that invariably gathers around a balloon.

Everyone pitches in to help unpack
and stretch out the nylon envelope.

All students are required to work with the ground
crew. There they learn important aspects of preflight
preparation, including the inflation of the envelope
and management of the fuel system. In addition, they
help on lift-offs, landings, deflation, and packing up
the balloon.

As such knowledge is being gained, the student also
gets in some flying time under the supervision of a
qualified instructor. Whoever the instructor is, perhaps the balloon's part owner and chief pilot, he or she
must hold a commercial certificate, which is needed to
teach.

60

Early flights may be safely tethered in order to give the student a feel for burner operations and the processes used to make the balloon ascend, descend, and land. Supervised free ballooning flights follow.

In time, if the instructor is satisfied that the student can operate the balloon in any situation, including an emergency, he may authorize a solo flight. Alone in the basket, high above the ground, the student has reached the end of his or her first phase of training.

During the two years that the student-pilot certificate remains in force, the new aeronaut may fly only under the supervision of an instructor. The student may not carry passengers or fly a balloon for hire. But in that time he gains experience and earns a basic certificate that is the first step on the road to becoming a licensed pilot.

A person must be at least sixteen years old to earn a pilot's license. The medical, language, and information requirements are the same as for students, but the private-certificate applicant also must take a written test dealing with the basic physics and mechanics of balloon flight. He or she must demonstrate a proficiency in the use of aeronautical charts, show a working knowledge of weather reports, and be able to recognize weather patterns and their potential effects upon an aerostat. Weather can be an aeronaut's friend or foe.

The applicant for a private-pilot certificate gets a considerable amount of ballooning experience. His or her logbook must show at least ten hours aloft in free-flight balloons. This time must further include six flights under supervision. Two of these flights must be at least thirty minutes long. One must be to an altitude of 3000 feet or more. The budding aeronaut also must successfully demonstrate competency during at least one solo flight that is being closely monitored from the ground.

Having earned a private-pilot's certificate, the new aeronaut is free to pursue ballooning alone or as part of a crew. But the private pilot still is not licensed to give flying lessons, carry paying passengers, or operate balloons for hire. Those areas of ballooning are open only to the commercial pilot.

The applicant for a commercial license must be at least eighteen years old and meet similar physical and language requirements to those of students and private pilots.

However, an applicant for a commercial license goes into all phases of balloon operations more deeply. An advanced written test covers the physics of flight. Strong emphasis is placed on passenger safety, navigation, weather forecasting, knowledge of wind patterns, cloud reading, and general meteorology. Of course, a commercial pilot must know all facets of ballooning from unpacking the envelope to flying, landing, and stowing the balloon.

Since commercial ballooning often involves contact with the public and may take place over populated areas, the pilot must demonstrate an ability to handle the crowds that so often gather around balloon operations. He or she must know how to protect both the balloon and landowner's property from harm. Experience has shown that most people are good-humored over infrequent visits by hot-air balloons. If a balloon makes a forced landing in a farmer's wheat field, he is usually mollified by the offer of a free ride and the acceptance of responsibility for any damage.

Commercial-pilot applicants (and private too) must demonstrate that they can perform certain maneuvers such as high-wind landings and water landings with particular skill. Since the maneuvering is done from within the balloon basket, the commercial-pilot trainee must spend at least thirty-five hours aloft. By the time the testing is finished, the applicant should be able to put the balloon through all of its moves with confidence, delicacy, and skill.

Typical of the maneuvers included in pilot testing is

the requirement for the trainee to put the balloon in a steady climb by using short bursts from the blast valve. Then he or she must level off and hold the altitude. In this way the pilot demonstrates the ability to maintain level flight with the burners as the balloon's air is cooling. Despite the availability of an altimeter and rate-of-climb indicator, a good pilot soon learns to fly the balloon "by the seat of his pants."

Temperature control also must be mastered by the commercial-certificate trainee. Prolonged overheating of a balloon envelope causes rapid deterioration and even charring of the fabric. Too little heat causes the balloon to descend rapidly; sometimes the descent is so rapid that the balloon bangs down to a bone-jarring landing before the fall can be checked. Accordingly, the trainee puts in at least ten flights in free balloons, a half-dozen of which are supervised by a veteran instructor who monitors each maneuver.

Within the advanced training period, the applicant makes several additional solo flights. Two must be for at least an hour's duration. Such lengthy flights afford time to practice cross-country navigation and careful fuel management, and they present a variety of conditions and problems that do not usually occur on shorter flights.

Safety is the primary concern of pilots in all three

Crew chief and pilot fuel and rig the basket
prior to attaching it to the envelope.

classes. They make sure that the balloon is thoroughly
inspected at least once a year and that it is carefully
maintained. During a flight, they are alert to any
change in the weather.

Even though a pilot may have called in and received

favorable weather information from the Flight Service Station (FSS), weather is fickle. Conditions may change in a matter of minutes. A pilot should be able to read at least basic weather signs. Stratus clouds are flat or straight, cumulus are puffy, and cirrus are feathery and icy. They exist in many combinations of fractus (broken), alto (high), or nimbus (raincloud). There are no precise rules of weather, nor are there precise cloud formations or wind patterns. But a balloonist must have a general knowledge of what to expect from approaching fronts, varying temperatures, shifting winds, and other meteorological changes.

The wise balloonist will not leave the ground if the wind is blowing at more than ten miles per hour. Seven miles per hour is tricky enough during inflation and flight and particularly during landing. An important point to remember is that winds usually pick up as morning progresses and solar heat begins to stir the air. The aeronaut must also watch for rising thermals and treacherous downdrafts as they too will increase.

Ballooning, like any activity, needs to be practiced regularly in order to retain the essential sharpness and skills. To keep alert, a commercial pilot should have flown at least two hours within the month prior to carrying passengers or giving lessons. This flight should be properly entered in the pilot's logbook, which all airmen, including balloonists, must maintain.

During flight, the aeronaut should be sensitive to all sorts of safety factors. He or she must contend with the time lag that occurs between the pulling of the blast-valve handle and the effect of the additional hot air on the balloon's movement. This time lag can range from a few seconds to a half minute, depending largely upon the difference between the temperatures of the air inside and outside of the balloon. The greater the difference, the longer the fresh blast of heat takes to lift the balloon.

Accordingly, a pilot should maintain a positive buoyancy most of the time. The balloon should be inclined to rise rather than fall. It is much easier to spill air out through the maneuvering vent and start down than to blast hot air into the envelope and lift it.

A power failure while drifting along is another possible danger. The pilot must be prepared to deal with a burner flameout. A sudden gust of wind from an unexpected quarter, known as a wind sheer, may snuff out the pilot light. A fuel leak or a frozen regulator may cut off fuel to the burner and also cause a flameout. After taking whatever corrective action is needed, the aeronaut usually tries to reignite the pilot light with

The chase crew watches over its drifting charge.

a sparker or a lighter, whichever is more effective. Flameouts are rare, however, when fuel systems are properly adjusted and maintained free of moisture or other contaminants.

The pilot must also watch the tank and be sure to

switch to a full one before it goes dry. Whenever a fuel problem cannot be corrected in time, the balloon will descend at ever-increasing speed, and its occupants must brace for a hard jolt.

Fortunately, although a hot-air balloon that loses power or otherwise drops out of control is headed for a rough landing, pilot or passengers seldom suffer serious injury. Even if the balloon rips open in flight, the very friction of the air against the limp fabric of the trailing envelope slows the speed enough so the ground impact will be about the same as a normal parachute landing.

High-tension wires are perhaps the worst hazard to aeronauts. These days threatening power lines seem to be everywhere, and they are not always easy to see at a distance. They are strung along the sides of roads. They leap from pole to pole across fields. The worry is that most of them carry potentially lethal charges of electrical voltage.

While a balloon drifts safely several hundred feet above ground level (AGL), there is no problem with power lines. However, as soon as a pilot begins hedge hopping, which is a big part of the fun in hot-air ballooning, he or she must keep close watch on the wires, plan well ahead, and hit the blast valve early if a lift is needed to clear them.

A well-trained, hardworking ground crew is as essential as a pilot to a successful balloon flight. Usually, approximately a half-dozen people make up a ground crew, although there may be more or less. Ground crewing is frequently volunteer duty, with wives, husbands, good friends, or simply enthusiasts working side by side. The rewards are the opportunity for some balloon flights, some practical student training, and work toward pilot certification. If the operation involves club ownership and maintenance of the balloon, serving on the ground crew is part of the duties of each member. Crew members normally rotate from ground duty to aerial activity on a planned schedule.

The ground crew comes under the command of the pilot, but their actual functioning usually is directed by a crew chief. He or she may be an alternate pilot, an advanced student, or someone who has considerable experience in handling hot-air balloons. Such a person has the ability to organize and manage others.

Only through well-orchestrated teamwork can a balloon flight succeed. That teamwork begins around dawn, when unpacking gets under way, and doesn't end until after the balloon is safely down, folded, and properly stowed.

5

Preflight

Preparing a hot-air balloon for flight requires careful planning and procedure from both pilot and ground crew. When done skillfully, a balloon can be unpacked and made ready for lift-off in ten to fifteen minutes.

In order to take advantage of the still early-morning air, the operation usually begins about dawn. The pilot arrives at the launch site armed with the latest weather-forecasting data. He has already called the Flight Service Station or perhaps some other source for meteorological information. If the sky is clear, he is primarily interested in predictions concerning the strength and direction of the winds at various altitudes, for they will determine the course of his flight.

The launch site has been carefully chosen for its smooth surface, which must be large enough for the crew to lay out the balloon prior to inflation. Also the

Filling propane tanks before dawn.

site should be downwind and well away from trees, power lines, and other obstacles.

Over steaming cups of coffee, pilot and crew chief brief other crew members about their duties. The experienced members are assigned key positions and tasks. Other helpers, who may be passengers awaiting

flight or eager volunteers, are directed to the less critical chores.

Everyone turns to the task of unloading the balloon,
the basket, the propane tanks, and a sizeable collection
of support equipment and paraphernalia. This gear
includes the burners, flight instruments, leather gloves,
protective helmets, spark igniters, a sectional map of
the area, plus a regular street map, and perhaps the
traditional bottle of champagne to celebrate a successful flight. An especially important item is the boxed-in
portable fan used during the initial cold-inflation phase
of preparing the balloon for flight.

All hands lay to as the crew unrolls and spreads the
thin nylon envelope carefully over the ground, which

Laying out the envelope.

has been inspected and cleared of sharp or abrasive objects that could tear or puncture the fabric. Although the air is fairly quiet, the balloon is laid out with the crown pointed downwind. Thus, the envelope will not be inclined to sway or fold back upon itself during inflation.

Soon the envelope is spread out according to numbers marked on the gores. These numbers help prevent the crew from twisting the gores and load tapes. They also serve as guides to ensure that the balloon is laid out with the maneuvering vent down so it will provide access to the inside of the bag for inspection during the initial stage of cold-air inflation. A low vent also prevents air leakage during early inflation.

Crewmen then install and secure several full propane tanks in the basket. Next they tip the basket on its side, facing toward the flattened and closed mouth of the balloon. The pilot and crew chief mount the burner assembly on its load ring or frame and hook up the fuel lines. Then they sort out the steel cables or ropes, stretching from the load tapes, and attach each one to its proper basket bracket. The main balloon elements are now assembled.

With everything laid out horizontally, the time has come to begin breathing life into the balloon. One crew member stations himself beyond the apex of the en-

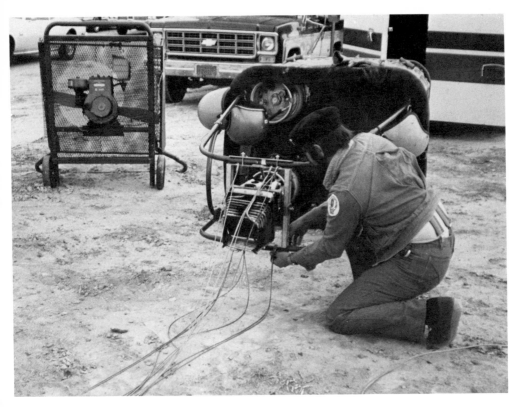

The pilot attaches the load cables to the basket frame,
which also supports the burner.

velope, prepared to handle the crown line stretched out
beyond the collapsed bag. Two other people take positions at the tangent ropes attached to load tapes on
opposite sides of the bag. These ropes will be used to
help spread and steady the balloon during inflation.

Using a small hand-held flint sparker, the crew chief
tests the burner system, both pilot light and main valve,
leaving it shut off. He then fires up the gasoline-
powered fan, or cold inflator, and signals two crew

A typical flint sparker for lighting the burner.

members to lift the edges and open up the balloon. Keeping clear of the load cables attached to the basket, they stretch open the mouth of the balloon so the inflator's airstream can be directed inside.

Slowly the envelope begins to swell under the force of the air fanned into it. It puffs up, forming a multicolored nylon cave with its floor still spread out on the ground. Now the pilot goes into the envelope through the maneuvering vent and makes a tour of the balloon's interior. He looks for holes or tears that might not have been detected earlier. Small holes the size of one's hand cause little worry, particularly if they are located low on the balloon. A larger hole near the crown where hot-air pressure is the greatest does cause concern and it might even be reason to cancel the flight.

Inflation begins by fanning cold air
into the open throat of the envelope.

With the fan inflator still blowing cold air into the envelope, the pilot checks the seal on the deflation port to be sure that the hooks and loops of the Velcro fastener are firmly meshed. While inside the crown, he inspects the telltales. They are small, heat-sensitive tabs that change color when they get too hot. Discoloration signals possible thermal damage to the envelope.

The pilot then looks at the maneuvering vent. He

pulls on the rope that opens the vent, releases it, and watches the pressure-activated seals snap shut. He makes sure that the red ripcord for the deflation port is hooked up and free from tangles. Turning to the thermocoupler also mounted inside the crown, he attaches the wire that will relay the temperature readings to the pyrometer in the basket.

Satisfied that everything inside the envelope is in airworthy condition, the pilot retreats toward the balloon's mouth. He takes the pyrometer wire, the rope for the maneuvering vent, and the deflation port ripcord with him, and he anchors each in its proper place in the gondola.

By now the balloon envelope has become about two-thirds inflated by the cool airstream from the fan. It lies on its side like a tired elephant, undecided whether or not to rise. The balloon rocks gently back and forth in the slight breeze, while members of the crew apply tension to the crown and side ropes to keep it from swaying or rolling over.

"O.K., let's hit her with some heat," the captain says, turning on the propane valve and lighting the pilot light with a spark from his igniter. Tilting the burner up a bit so that it points into the center of the balloon's open mouth, he checks to see that load cables, ropes, the protective fabric skirt around the mouth, and the envelope itself are clear.

Now the pilot pulls the blast-valve handle. With a roar, the blueish flame from the burner stabs through the balloon's gaping mouth and begins to heat the air. After a few such bursts, the temperature inside the envelope increases, and the bag struggles to rise from the ground. The captain turns off the inflator fan and sets it back out of the way.

"Hold 'er down!" The message is relayed to the rope handlers. To allow the envelope to tilt up vertically before it is fully buoyant could set up a dangerous twisting oscillation or even cause the balloon to roll over. So crewmen put extra tension on the lines to hold the balloon down despite its inclination to rear up-right.

The pilot continues directing bursts from the burner into the still-swelling envelope. Then, above the roar of the blasts, he motions to the crew chief standing off to one side.

"Ease off!" the crew chief shouts, and signals with his hands to the rope handlers. The helpers on each side of the balloon relax the tension on the lines, but they do not let go.

The pilot puts one more blast of hot air into the en-

A crewmember steadies the crown line
to prevent oscillation of the partially inflated balloon.

velope. "Ease off on the crown," he shouts. The far-
thest crewman relaxes tension on the crown line, and
the expanding envelope strains to lift itself.

"Let her up!" the pilot calls. All hands turn loose.
Unrestrained, the bulging bag heaves off the ground

and sways to an upright position. As it rises, it tilts the basket upright, and the pilot quickly steps inside so there is no chance of the balloon taking off without him. Others rush forward, ready to lean on the basket rim to help hold it down if necessary.

The gathered spectators gaze in awe at the colorful sphere straining skyward.

Using the burner carefully to hot-inflate the balloon.

With everything weighted down and under control, the crew chief climbs into the basket with the pilot. Together they set about checking out the system and equipment. They must be sure everything needed is at hand and operating properly before lift-off: a ten-inch adjustable wrench, a screwdriver, a spare spark igniter in case one should malfunction. The pilot pats his pockets to reassure himself that he has the extra matches and lighter that might come in handy if all else fails. Fire is the heartbeat of a hot-air balloon. In case of a flameout or other loss of burner heat, there must be a way to relight.

The crew chief sees that the fifty- to a hundred-foot-long ground-handling rope is aboard and that there is a protective helmet for each scheduled occupant of the gondola. He checks that proper area maps are in the holder and that the FAA-approved airworthiness and aircraft-registration certificates are there.

The pilot checks the tank gauges to be sure he is carrying a full load of propane. He sets the fuel-pressure regulator and makes a final inspection of the valves and hoses for possible leaks. They usually show up as frost spots caused by the supercold vaporization of escaping gas.

Then he turns to the instrument package hanging inside the basket rim. Referring to the barometric-pressure figure provided earlier by the FSS, he now sets the altimeter so it will give him correct altitude readings throughout the flight. The needle of the rate-of-climb indicator is set at neutral O. The pilot taps the pyrometer and decides that it shows the correct temperature of the heated air near the crown of the balloon. It seems a bit low, so he yanks the blast-valve handle to put a little more hot air into the envelope to keep it from sagging.

At this point, he secures the control line dropping down from the maneuvering vent and the red line from the deflation port. Each must be within easy reach, yet free from accidental entanglement.

With the crew members leaning on the basket to hold it down, the pilot quickly reviews the flight plan. He points to a layer of high cumulus clouds. They portend a weather change, but the FSS has indicated that the front is still a day or so away. The winds aloft seem to be moving in a westerly direction, although there is always the possibility that they could shift without warning.

The pilot searches his pockets for a few nickels and dimes in case he needs to make a phone call after landing. He and the crew chief settle on a common number to call in case they lose visual and radio contact with each other. Landings sometimes take place behind

Balloons mushroom from a desert airport prior to lift-off.

mountains or far away from access roads, and someone has to go in search of a telephone. Finally, the crew chief makes sure that he, not the pilot, has the key to the chase vehicle!

Now all checks have been made. The support equipment used during assembly and inflation of the balloon is gathered up and stowed in the chase vehicle.

Everything is in order for the launching.

6

Fly With Me

Ever since catching sight of the first rainbow-hued hot-air balloon drifting languidly overhead, you have longed to share the experience. Now your turn has come.

The crew chief vaults out of the basket and nods for you to climb aboard. Careful not to become entangled in the dangling ropes and assorted paraphernalia hanging from the gondola, you scramble over the padded edge and take up a vacant corner in the basket. The pilot glances up from checking a valve and smiles a welcome.

There is little spare standing room amidst the three upright propane tanks, the coil of rope, the instrument package, and the valves, hoses, wires, and connecting straps. You bang an elbow on one of the safety helmets dangling over the basket edge.

"We may need them later if we have a rough landing," the pilot explains. "Just make yourself comfortable." He chuckles, knowing full well that the small basket provides few creature comforts. Then he points to the inch-wide red strap hanging down into the basket from somewhere high up inside the balloon.

"Just don't touch that ripcord," he warns. "It opens the deflation port and spills the hot air. That's something we don't want to do until we're landing and need to collapse the envelope. Repeat. Hands off the ripcord."

You nod. "Don't worry," you add, by way of assurance.

While the pilot busily checks this and adjusts that, the air inside the balloon cools off somewhat. Even when the crew members ease their weight off the rim, the basket remains solidly on the ground.

"Let's weigh off," the pilot says. He opens the blast valve for a five-second burst, then closes it for a few seconds. Nothing happens. Again he sends a long tongue of yellow-blue flame up into the bulging bag.

You sense a slight tug on the basket.

"Ease off," the pilot orders.

Lift-off!

Drifting languidly over the countryside.

Without letting go completely, the crew further relaxes its hold on the basket rim. You feel definite motion as the gondola lifts a few inches, then drops gently back to the ground. The pilot looks tentatively toward the sky, taking note of the sudden sway and lean of the balloon envelope overhead. Worry lines furrow his forehead.

"We'd better check the winds again," he says to his crew chief. "Let's get the guinea pig."

The crewman trots over to the chase vehicle and returns with a toy gas-filled balloon brought from home —the guinea pig used for testing the wind. He turns it loose. All eyes watch it climb a slanting path into the sky, noting the direction and speed of its movement. The pilot whistles softly as he watches the tiny balloon skim over a row of trees bordering a nearby roadway.

"We'll want plenty of lift," he says, more to himself than to you. He spaces out a couple of more yanks on the blast valve. "It's a lot better to use a series of short bursts than a single long one," he explains. "It allows time for the hot air to spread out in the bag and not overheat the fabric."

He looks at the pyrometer, which indicates a temperature near the crown of slightly over 200 degrees Fahrenheit. "About right. We try to keep the temperature as low as our payload will allow so as to preserve the fabric."

You've already learned that the cooler the weather, the less heat is required inside the balloon to establish the needed lift. One hundred degrees between inside and outside temperature is usually sufficient to lift the balloon. There are, of course, many variables to be considered, such as the size of the envelope, the weight of the payload, and burner output, before the right flight formula can be established. In this area, pilot experience is often more dependable than slide-rule calculation.

"Let's weigh off," the pilot says once more. Again the crew members ease their grip on the basket rim. The gondola makes a positive movement upward, but not quite fast enough to please the balloon captain. "Pull her down again!"

He reaches again for the blast valve, explaining, "That's not bad buoyancy, but we'd better have a little extra insurance in case we drift toward those trees."

Looking past the flame, you see that the first sunbeams have reached the balloon. They shine through the colored fabric, backlighting the inside of the envelope like a stained-glass window.

"Everybody clear?" the pilot calls, having noticed the growing ranks of spectators, who have appeared magically out of the dawn.

"Back, folks, please," the crew chief calls. Then he signals, "All's clear!"

"OK. Hands off!"

Those who have been pressing down on the rim let go and step back away from the basket. Once again the pilot reaches for the blast valve.

Whoo-oosh-hh!

The roar echoes through the morning air. The pilot holds the valve open for about four seconds, then releases it.

Silence.

You don't really feel any movement as you watch the people steadily shrink to the size of toy soldiers. Could the earth and the people be moving, not you? It surely seems that way. You lean farther out to get a better look downward. The wicker basket creaks under your shifting weight and snaps you back to reality.

The balloon drifts languidly some twenty feet above the ground. A sudden shift of air currents sends it careering toward the trees.

Whoo-oosh-hh! The pilot gives the burner another four-second blast. But the balloon doesn't respond immediately, and the trees loom closer.

"Hold tight," the veteran aeronaut warns. "We've got a ten- to fifteen-second time lag before that hot air spreads out and gives some lift to the balloon."

You wait, eyeing the trees anxiously. After what seems an eternity, the balloon rises in response to the burner fire. The treetops slip away beneath the basket, almost close enough for you to reach out and grab.

The aeronaut then begins a series of short burns, which causes the balloon to rise in almost imperceptible steps to a height of five hundred feet as indicated on the altimeter. By this time the pilot spaces out the burns, watching the pyrometer and adding just enough heat to compensate for the natural cooling inside the envelope. Having reached its equilibrium, the balloon maintains its level as it drifts with the breeze.

Balanced between land and sky, the colorful aerostat seems suspended in space. You sense a strange stillness. Not even a breeze brushes your face to indicate movement.

"Oh, there's a breeze around us," the pilot comments, "maybe five or six miles per hour. But it's carrying us right along. We're matching speed with it, so we can't feel it."

Moving slowly and effortlessly, you have no sense of going anyplace. You need a point of reference. You look down over the rim of the basket and take a sighting on a red-roofed barn. As you watch, it appears to drift slowly westward. Clearly the balloon is moving east in the grip of a mild westerly breeze.

A rooster crows. Chased by the balloon's shadow, a cottontail darts for cover. You spot a crow flying beneath you. Drifting slowly, you have plenty of time to see and hear everything going on all around you. There is no sense of speed or blurring of landscape as you get from a low-flying airplane.

A little farther on, a young couple alerted by their barking dog step out of their front door. They look up, spot you, and wave. You wave back and exchange greetings. Then you focus your camera on them and snap a picture. Almost everyone who rides a hot-air balloon carries a camera. It's part of the fun of sport ballooning.

"Let's try it up a little higher for a while," the pilot suggests, as you continue drifting slowly downwind.

Using short burner bursts, the aeronaut lifts the balloon, frequently checking the pyrometer to be sure the temperature inside the envelope remains well below the red-line maximum. The variometer indicates a climbing rate of six hundred feet per minute. Yet you feel little sensation other than a slight pressure on the soles of your feet, like standing in a rising elevator.

By deft use of the burner, the pilot trims the craft and levels off at fifteen hundred feet. He checks the fuel gauges and turns a couple of valves while switching to a full tank.

"We've caught a different breeze at this altitude," he says. "It oftens happens. Sometimes you can go almost where you want. By searching at different altitudes, you can hitchhike on a wind moving in the right direction."

You hadn't noticed any change in course, but now you look down and see the smoke from a factory chimney definitely bending eastward. By sighting on a tree, you can see that the balloon is drifting southwestward, in almost the opposite direction from the ground wind.

"With a little luck, we might go back almost to our launch site," the pilot says. "That would sure please the chase crew. But this doesn't look like a very good landing area."

You look down and off to the side about a mile. The chase vehicle is a small red-and-white camper, towing a boxlike trailer painted in matching colors. It has been

The chase crew tries to keep within visual or radio contact of the free-flying aerostat.

During a breezy touchdown,
pilot and crew have their hands full.

in sight during most of the flight. Every once in a while
you have seen it stop while someone got out, looked up,
and apparently tried to determine just where the balloon was drifting. A couple of times during low-level
flight the balloon had settled behind a ridge, and the
chase vehicle had disappeared from sight and dropped
out of radio range.

"They go a little bananas when they lose us," the
pilot explains. "And we can use their help when we
land. Also, if I decide to make a touch-and-go landing

to let you off and pick up new passengers, the chase vehicle carries the spare fuel tanks so I can continue flying."

At the moment you're enjoying drifting through the sky so much that you don't want to think of landing. You marvel at the scenery. Except for the occasional roar of the burner, it is silent. How delightful to be disconnected from the earth for an hour or so! You feel a certain euphoria, a pleasant hypnotism. No, you don't want to land. Not yet, anyway.

"Where are we going?" you ask, hopeful that the pilot is not seriously thinking of descending.

"With the wind," he replies, smiling, and reaches once more for the blast valve. "With the wind."

7

The Landing

Inevitably the time arrives to bring the balloon down. The most favorable landings are made in calm weather in areas free of watery or upthrusting obstacles and conveniently close to an access road. Roadside landings enable the chase crew to be on hand to assist in handling ropes and snugging the balloon down safely.

If the landing is to exchange passengers, the balloon will not be deflated, but simply weighted down and steadied until the new passengers are in the basket. The pilot may trade empty propane tanks for full ones at the same time. He then blasts more heat into the balloon and lifts off again.

However, if the morning's flying is finished, and the balloon is to be deflated and dismantled, landing close to a road saves the crew from having to carry the heavy tanks, bag, basket, and other equipment long distances

Using a hand gauge to check surface winds prior to a flight.

to the chase vehicle. Unfortunately, roadside landings and threatening wires seem to go together, so the wise pilot keeps a safe downwind distance from the wires, regardless of how far the disassembled balloon parts may have to be carried.

Throughout the flight, the aeronaut, like the pilot of any airborne vehicle, must always think ahead. Above all, he or she must have a potential landing area in mind or preferably in sight. Anticipation and planning make for a successful flight.

When approaching a freshly plowed field on a hot

The pilot chooses a likely landing site well ahead of time.

day, an alert balloon pilot anticipates a rising thermal of warm air, which will lift the balloon to a higher altitude. Crossing a lake or a green field at low altitude, he knows the balloon may descend in a cool downdraft. The changes may not be felt in the basket, but the rate-of-climb indicator shows the shift.

The balloonist picks a landing area relatively free of tall trees, buildings, heavy traffic, or clusters of people. Once it has been chosen, he has limited means at his disposal to reach it. Again anticipation plays a major role. Is the breeze blowing toward the site, and will it hold its direction all the way to the ground? The pilot may drop a scrap of paper over the side and watch it drift toward the earth. If it changes direction on its downward path, probably the balloon will do the same. So the pilot changes altitude in order to accommodate the expected variation in wind direction. Thus, he avoids undershooting or overshooting the field.

While descending, he checks the smoke from a chimney, the amount of flutter in a flag, or even the movement of rustling leaves across the ground. There are many ways to determine the strength and direction of the surface winds.

The pilot takes all of these things into consideration, and he decides on a landing plan that will make them work for him. He adjusts his altitude carefully, since it is his main method of control. Horizontal movement is mostly determined by the power of the breeze. If the pilot thinks that the slowly descending balloon will overshoot the field, he pulls the maneuvering vent line in order to spill a little air and increase the rate of descent.

During landing, the pilot of even a slow-drifting balloon is kept quite busy. If he doesn't have the time to do everything himself, he directs a passenger to help with the prelanding tidying up. Loose tools, gloves, extra cameras, sparkers, thermos jugs, and any other gear that might have been put aboard prior to lift-off are stowed or fastened down. Someone checks that the ground-handling rope is out of its bag and ready to be lowered over the side at the pilot's order.

With everything prepared, the pilot maneuvers the balloon as best he can toward the selected touchdown spot. In calm weather he can pretty well control the descent with the blast valve and the maneuvering vent, judging the drift and adjusting the distance by raising or lowering the balloon's altitude.

The closer the balloon is to the ground, the more easily the pilot can judge the all-important movement of air currents. Faced with flying dust or swaying tree branches, he knows he is in for a potentially rough landing. He orders those around him to put on a protective helmet and slip on the available gloves to prevent abrasions.

On the ground, the chase vehicle is moving ahead on a dirt road toward the anticipated landing spot. Judging the breeze to be about fifteen miles per hour, the pilot knows he is going to need their help. He eases the balloon down to about one hundred feet; then he checks the descent with several blasts from the burner. He wants to maintain positive buoyancy—to be ascending, not descending—as he crosses over the high-tension wires strung along the road.

As the basket floats safely over the power lines, the pilot tugs on the maneuvering-vent cord for a couple of seconds, spilling out hot air, then releases it. Far up in the balloon, the vent automatically snaps shut. The balloon drifts toward the open field at a shallow downward angle.

"Throw out the towline," the pilot instructs. One end of the rope uncoils toward the members of the chase crew, who have left their vehicle parked at the edge of the road and now run along beneath the breeze-borne balloon.

"We may get dragged a bit," the pilot cautions the others. "Stand at the back of the basket and face the direction we'll be landing. When we hit the ground, bend your knees to absorb the shock. If we bounce or tip on our side, stay with the basket unless I order you out. The ground crew should be able to hold us. If we drag, it won't be for long."

By now the balloon is down to an altitude of fifty feet. Scrambling over rocks and through weed patches, the chase crew is having difficulty getting a good grasp on the dangling rope. But the pilot sees his best landing spot directly ahead. The cooling balloon continues its gentle windblown descent. Satisfied that all is going well, the pilot reaches down and shuts off the main propane feed valve. Now he takes a firm grip on the red ripcord leading to the deflation port.

"Brace yourselves," he warns, closely judging the distance from the ground in relation to the forward speed of the balloon.

Just as the balloon touches down, the pilot yanks hard on the ripcord. Far overhead the Velcro seal tears apart, spilling air out the large hole in the crown. The basket thumps along the ground, bounces once, and begins skidding as the collapsing envelope forms a breeze-driven sail. By now, though, the crewmen have a firm grip on the ground line and a couple of the side lines, and one man is running forward to grab the crown line and pull the bag downwind as it collapses.

At the last moment, the basket topples over on its side. The dragging has ceased, and after noting that most of the air has spilled from the envelope the pilot signals for the slightly shaken passengers to crawl from the basket. They do so, smiling broadly as they brush themselves off.

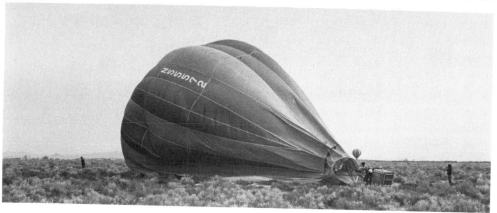

Top: At touchdown the pilot yanks the ripcord,
and the balloon begins to collapse.
Bottom: The collapsing balloon lies on its side.

104

The bag sighs as it continues to deflate and settle over the ground like a limp sail.

Now everyone starts to dismantle the balloon and pack away the parts. The ground crew bend to their separate tasks, while the spectators who gathered at the sight of the descending balloon stand by to lend a hand if needed.

The pilot detaches the load cables that connect the basket to the collapsed balloon. Working from the mouth toward the crown of the balloon, several crew members gather the limp fabric into a lengthwise yard-wide strip stretched out on the ground. In the process, they tuck handling lines and perhaps decorative banners into the folds. Once they reach the crown and squeeze out the last small bubble of air, the pilot and a helper carefully reseal the Velcro lips of the deflation port so it will be ready for the next flight.

With the fabric laid out in a neat compact strip, several crew members begin at the crown to fold and cram the material into a large canvas storage bag. As they work toward the mouth of the balloon, they inspect the fabric, remove twigs, brush off dirt, and note any holes that may have been punctured or burned in the envelope.

With the balloon stuffed into the canvas bag, one of

Squeezing out the last of the air.

the crew places the burner frame and coiled load cables gently on top of it, then pulls the drawstring tight to seal the bag. The compact package weighs more than two hundred pounds.

Meanwhile, having tipped the wicker basket back upright, the pilot disconnects the fuel lines and lifts the empty or partially filled propane tanks over the side to be carried to the chase vehicle. He then carefully disconnects the instrument package and puts it into a protective box with the disassembled burner. Both delicate parcels need special handling.

Stuffing the bulky envelope into its carrying bag
is a job for all hands.

Several crew members team up to carry the empty
basket to the chase vehicle. Then they return for the
sacked nylon envelope.

When everything is securely tucked away in the
trailer, all hands scour the landing site to be sure no
tools or equipment are left behind. They pick up debris
and rake over scuff marks at the same time, wanting to
leave the area clean and neat. If they have landed on
private property and the owner is at hand, they make a
definite effort to show their appreciation. Quite often

Everything is gathered up and put away.

they offer the person a free balloon ride on some future launch.

Then the crew breaks out the champagne. This tradition began nearly two hundred years ago when the first aeronauts carried wine to placate superstitious peasants who often were angered or frightened by balloons dropping out of the sky. Today the champagne marks the end of a pleasant flight. Newly baptized aeronauts talk over their venture. Usually they receive a certificate testifying that they have severed earthly bonds and ascended high into the heavens in a hot-air balloon. They have had an experience they will long remember.

The author receives his certificate
after his first balloon flight.

8
At Work and Play

During recent years, hot-air balloons have attracted the greatest interest. Such balloons are comparatively inexpensive, simple to operate, can be used commercially, and above all they're fun.

Only a handful of aeronauts hope to make a profit from their balloons, yet some do by carrying passengers on free flights or tethered rides. Perhaps the curious or adventuresome have seen ads or had friends tell them what a great experience ballooning is. By Saturday morning a commercial balloonist may find a dozen or more passengers signed up for rides. In an AX-7 class balloon, which can handle over nine hundred pounds of payload, the pilot can carry three passengers at a time and still maintain a good safety margin of lift. With fifteen passengers, the pilot must land the balloon five times in order to let off and pick up people following the chase vehicle.

During a couple of the landings, the crew must replace nearly empty fuel tanks. Depending upon conditions, three ten-gallon propane tanks provide approximately two hours of flying time. But for safety, the tanks should be exchanged for full ones before they run dry.

Providing a stiff breeze doesn't arise and put an early halt to the day's ballooning, an aeronaut can have a profitable morning. His charge per passenger may range anywhere from twenty-five to eighty dollars for a half hour's ballooning.

A hot-air balloonist also may hire out his aerostat and himself as pilot for a wide variety of promotional events. A hot-air balloon may deliver Santa Claus to a shopping center. Carnival promoters sometimes hire a balloon to carry parachutists aloft to jump and attract a crowd. But the most common advertising use of hot-air balloons is converting them into flying billboards. Many large companies buy their own balloons and hire aeronauts to fly and maintain them. Others simply sponsor a balloonist, take care of expenses, and pay a fee to have their name or product displayed from the sky. Attention is guaranteed; almost everyone looks up at a colorful balloon passing overhead.

Most of the profit from ballooning, however, probably goes back into fuel and maintainence of the bag

Unmanned balloons of all sizes and designs
serve scientific purposes.

and basket. The balloon also must undergo either an
annual or a 100-hour flight-time inspection and maintenance check as required by the FAA. This thorough
going over is performed for a fee by a licensed profes-
sional inspector. At the same time, balloon owners put
money away toward the purchase of a new envelope
sometime in the future. Heat and ultraviolet rays slowly
deteriorate a balloon, and in general, an envelope needs
replacement after about 400 hours of service. A new
envelope costs thousands of dollars.

Novelty balloons are featured in many parades.

A hot-air balloon sometimes takes on a shape
to fit its particular commercial purpose.

Therefore, while there is such a thing as ballooning
for profit, most hot-air ballooning is done for the fun
and adventure of it.

114

Aeronauts gather for competitive fun.

Balloonists, like all sportsmen, are keen to pit their skills against one another. Accordingly, an entire catalog of events has been developed to determine who is the best aeronaut at any given time. These events usually take place during mass launches, when balloonists gather at some suitable spot on desert, plain, or prairie to demonstrate their airworthiness.

One challenging event is a time-distance race. Pilot and crew start to inflate the balloon at a given signal, then lift off and go as far as possible and land within an hour's time. Less simple than it sounds, the winner usually is the one who prepares most carefully, studies the weather, and has the skill to find favorable winds. Credit also must be given to the crew's ability to get the balloon airborne quickly and without mishap.

Another lively event is known as hare and hounds. The hare balloon takes off ahead of the hounds. It lands several miles away. Whichever of the hound balloons catches up and lands closest to the hare wins the event.

There also are altitude-control contests, in which the aeronaut follows a preset up-and-down pattern. He or she must be able to ascend, level off, or descend with precision. This exercise requires a steady hand on the blast valve and a knowledge of the balloon's sensitivity to cooling or the ingestion of hot air. The pilot must be

The hare leaves a telltale trail for the hounds to follow.

able to use the blast valve and the maneuvering vent with equal skill.

Then there is the bomb drop. First the aeronaut maneuvers over a target, perhaps a big X on the ground, then drops a weighted marker as near as possible to it. In this event, the aeronaut must be able to make proper use of the winds to be in the running, and a favorable launch site is one at a reasonable upwind

117

Such stunts as launching hang gliders
from a hot-air balloon are for experts only.

distance from the target. Sometimes a crowd of competing balloonists can create a wild scramble for prime spots.

One version of the bomb drop calls for releasing a tumbleweed from an altitude of 500 feet, where the winds are likely to toss it back and forth in every direction except toward the target. In another version the flier is asked to ease a gondola down to within ten feet of a golf-course green and then try to drop a hole in one.

One very profitable demonstration of precision ballooning took place at a recent meet sponsored by the Balloon Federation of America (BFA), the National Aeronautic Association, and the worldwide Fédération Aeronautique Internationale. The contest took place during one of the biggest of all hot-air-ballooning get-togethers, the International Hot-Air Ballooning Fiesta held in Albuquerque, New Mexico. A free four-wheel-drive vehicle was offered to any aeronaut who could maneuver his or her balloon close enough to a twenty-foot pole to pick the keys to the car off the tip of it.

One pilot went to a great deal of trouble studying maps, checking weather, and choosing direction. Just before launch, he released several small helium-filled guinea-pig balloons and closely watched their direction and angle of ascent. Then, with the help of an all-girl ground crew, he inflated the balloon and lifted off. As he climbed, the pilot spit over the side now and then, watched the direction of the saliva, and made minor adjustments with his burners and maneuvering vent. His care and planning paid off when at a precise moment during his drifting flight he reached out and snatched the keys off the pole, making the vehicle his very own.

But nothing exceeds the thrill of participating in, or even watching, a mass launch as dozens of hot-air balloons lift from the ground and drift through the sky. These events occur periodically in many parts of the nation when a group of balloonists get together in one place. A fine show takes place in Indianola, Iowa, where the National Championships are held each August, and an even grander display can be seen during the World Championships.

Perhaps the most poignant demonstration of hot-air ballooning occurred in 1979. Two East German families, the Strelczyks and the Wetzels, secretly constructed a very large hot-air balloon capable of carrying four adults and four children. Late on the night of September 15, after checking wind directions and speed, they transported the balloon to a barren hilltop outside of their small town.

Using a large fan powered by a loudly barking motorcycle engine, they started to inflate the great envelope. Nobody in the area paid any attention, al-

Freedom of flight is the main purpose of ballooning.

though they made a lot of noise. Within twenty minutes the partially filled envelope rolled restlessly on the ground. In an additional fifteen minutes, hot air from the burner tilted the bag upright. With eight people clinging to the roughly constructed platform that served as a gondola, the balloon lifted slowly into the darkness.

Soaring up to frigid heights of over eight thousand feet in order to escape the probing searchlights, they drifted quietly over the border and landed twenty-eight minutes later in West Germany—escapees from Communism.

Hot-air ballooning seems to offer something different to everybody—fun, adventure, even freedom.

Glossary

aeronaut—balloonist.

aerostat—balloon, lighter-than-air vehicle.

aerostation—the art of ballooning.

altimeter—altitude indicator.

apex—*see* crown.

bag—*see* envelope.

balloon—lighter-than-air craft filled with gas or hot air.

Balloon Federation of America (BFA)—official organization of ballooning in America. Sanctioned by National Aeronautic Association and Fédération Aeronautique Internationale.

basket—the load-carrying part of a balloon.

blast valve—a hand-operated valve that controls fuel flow to burners.

blimp—elongated airship, usually nonrigid.

burner—assembly for mixing propane fuel and air to produce flame.

burner frame—metalwork on which burner is mounted above basket.

captive balloon—a balloon tethered to the ground.

ceiling—the altitude at which inner and outer densities equalize, and balloon levels off.

Charlier—a gas-filled balloon (named for Jacques Charles).

crown—top center of balloon.

crown line—rope stretched from apex to prevent oscillation of balloon during inflation.

cruise valve—a metered valve to adjust fuel flow.

deflation line—*see* ripcord.

deflation port—opening in crown for rapid escape of hot air.

dirigible—a powered aerostat capable of being steered.

drift—lateral motion of an airship.

122

envelope—the main part of the balloon filled with gas or hot air.

equilibrium—state in which balloon is stable, neither ascending nor descending.

Federal Aviation Administration (FAA)—the Government regulatory agency of all aviation activity.

free balloon—an untethered aerostat.

gondola—*see* basket.

gore—a fabric section of the balloon.

hands off—traditional order for ground crew to release the balloon.

helium—second lightest gas, nonflammable.

hydrogen—lightest element and gas, flammable.

inflator—usually a powered fan used for preliminary ground inflation.

lighter-than-air craft—*see* balloon.

load tapes—reinforced tapes along seams and around balloon to take the weight and relieve pressure from the fabric.

logbook—aeronaut's record of ballooning activity.

maneuvering vent—self-sealing aperture for controlled release of hot air.

Montgolfier—common name for hot-air balloon.

payload—what a balloon carries.

preflight—inspection prior to flight.

propane—liquified petroleum gas (LPG) used as burner fuel.

pyrometer—instrument that measures temperature in crown of balloon.

rally—gathering of balloons for fun and sport.

red line—maximum temperature not to be exceeded, usually 250°-300°F.

ripcord—a coded red tape to activate deflation port.

rip panel—see deflation port.

skirt—extra shroud around mouth of balloon to protect burner from wind gusts.

solo—flying alone.

step climb—ascending by series of short climbs.

suspension wires—cables that connect load tapes to gondola.

telltale—heat-sensitive device set in crown of balloon to warn if envelope has been exposed to damaging high temperatures.

temperature differential—difference between inside and outside air.

tether—a rope or line anchoring balloon to ground.

touch-and-go—lift-off and landing without full stop, part of training.

trim—when lift balances gravity, the balloon attains neutral buoyancy.

variometer—vertical speed indicator.

weigh off—balloon rises gently under a small amount of positive buoyancy.

*indicates illustration

125

helium, *See* gas, helium
Hindenburg, the, 31
history of ballooning, *See*
  ballooning, history of
hydrogen, *See* gas, hydrogen
indicator, vertical speed, *See*
  variometer
inflation process, 75-81*, 77*,
  80*, 84*
inflator, cold, 73, 75-79, 77*,
  120, 123
instructor, 60-61, 64
instrument package, 39, 41, 52-
  53*, 73, 82-83, 85, 106
International Hot-Air Ballooning
  Fiesta (Albuquerque, New
  Mexico), 119
Jeffries, Dr. John, 24
landing, 60, 63, 97-103, 99*,
  104*, 105-109, 106*
launch site, 71-72, 94, 117-118
launches, mass, 116-120
Lawler, Brian, 8
license, pilot's, 60-64
lift-off, 60, 71, 82, 86*
lighter-than-air (LTA) craft,
  10, 13
logbook, 66-67, 123
Los Angeles, the, 29
Louis XVI of France, 16-17, 21
Lowe, Professor Thaddeus, 26
LPG, *See* gas, propane
Luftschiff Zeppelin No. 1 (LZ-1),
  27-28
manned balloon flight, first, 17,
  19, 21

manufacturers, balloon, 8, 38-39,
  43
maps, 54, 73, 82, 119
Montgolfier, 12*, 14-17, 19, 21
Montgolfier, Joseph and
  Étienne, 13-17, 19
Napoleon, 26
National Aeronautic Association,
  119, 122
National Air and Space Museum
  (Washington, D.C.), 34, 36
National Championships
  (Indianola, Iowa), 120
packing balloon, 60, 105-106,
  107*, 108*
passengers, 8, 41, 55, 61, 66,
  72-73, 95-96, 97, 103, 110
payload, 46, 89-90, 110, 123
"phlogiston," *See* gas, hydrogen
Picard, Don, 8
Pilâtre de Rozier, François, 17,
  19, 21
pilot, 7-8, 13, 46, 48, 53-54,
  56-58, 60-70, 65*, 71-72,
  74, 75*, 76-84, 85, 87-96,
  95*, 97-103, 99*, 104*,
  105-106, 116, 119-120
pilot light, 50, 67-68, 78
power failure (flameout), 67-68,
  82
power lines, 69, 71-72, 98, 102
preflight, 60, 71-84*, 72*, 73*,
  75*, 76*, 77*, 80*, 81*,
  123
profit from ballooning, 61-62,
  110-112, 114*

127